CONTEMPORARY WRITERS IN CHRISTIAN PERSPECTIVE
EDITED BY RODERICK JELLEMA

William Styron

A CRITICAL ESSAY
BY ROBERT H. FOSSUM

WILLIAM B. EERDMANS / PUBLISHER

Quotations from William Styron's *Lie Down in Darkness* are reprinted by permission of The Bobbs-Merrill Co., copyright 1951, by William Styron.

Quotations from the following books by William Styron are reprinted by permission of Random House, Inc.: *The Long March*, copyright 1952, by William Styron; *Set This House on Fire*, copyright 1959, 1960, by William Styron; *The Confessions of Nat Turner*, copyright 1966, 1967, by William Styron.

To

my mother and the memory of my father

ACKNOWLEDGMENTS

My thanks are due William Styron and Robert D. Loomis, editor at Random House, who graciously sent me an advance copy of *The Confessions of Nat Turner*; The National Foundation on the Arts and Humanities for a summer fellowship which made the writing of this booklet possible; Claremont Men's College for typing funds; and Mrs. Catherine Tramz and Mrs. Grace Scherer, who helped with the final preparation of the manuscript. My deepest debt of gratitude is as always to Gigi, Kris, Rob, and Beth for reminding me, by their presence and their love, that there are things more important than scholarship.

—R.H.F.

Claremont Men's College
Claremont, California

CONTENTS

5

In his provocative little book, *Four Spiritual Crises in Mid-Century American Fiction,* Robert Detweiler remarks that America's post-World War II generation "has produced novelists who are more vitally and directly concerned with religion in fiction than any preceding age." If true, then we are faced with a curious state of affairs indeed: that a culture so scientistic, comfort-loving, and joylessly hedonistic as to be labeled "post-Christian" should produce writers who take religion "earnestly and objectively enough to render it an integral part of their creations." Yet when one thinks of novelists such as Flannery O'Connor, William Styron, J. D. Salinger, and John Updike, it is clear that Detweiler is quite right. Although our better writers tend largely to share the characteristic American suspicion of systematic theology and institutionalized faith, they also seem to share Gunnar Urang's feeling that America is suffering from a disease of the spirit which "cries out for a religious interpretation, an interpretation in terms of finitude, anxiety, sin, guilt, despair, grace, repentance, faith, regeneration, and eschatological interpretation." These are certainly the terms, along with others gleaned from Freud and the Existentialists, implicit in William Styron's fictional treatments of our current plight. He has published only four books so far, including the recent and highly praised *The Confessions of Nat Turner.* But all four reveal his concern with what Tillich calls questions of the "ultimate and the unconditional." The first three depict the spiritual vacuity of our age and the desperate measures men adopt in an effort to fill it. The last suggests that no historical period can claim to have cornered the market on these dubious commodities. And all four demonstrate, as David Galloway says, that a writer can "express despair without succumbing to it," that he can "deny the validity of traditional consolations without denying the traditions of the human spirit."

7

Fathers and Children: "Lie Down in Darkness"

—"Behold, we have not been brought up right."

Styron's first novel, *Lie Down in Darkness* (1951), brought the then twenty-six-year-old author the Prix de Rome of the American Academy of Arts and Letters. It won for him the praise of such critics as Maxwell Geismar, Howard Mumford Jones, and Alfred Kazin. And it put him, inevitably, into the class of "promising young novelists." Less happily, it also immediately stamped the native Virginian (who now lives with his wife and three children in Roxbury, Connecticut) with the label "Southern Novelist." Begun while Styron was studying writing at Duke with William Blackburn, the novel was not finished until the young Southerner had moved to New York and come under the influence of Hiram Haydn. Still, it was set in a Virginia town obviously based on Newport News, Styron's home town. Moreover, its style—Styron has subsequently described it as "self-conscious" and "ornate"—was clearly an example of Southern Rhetoric. Its occasional hyperbole inevitably invoked the name of Thomas Wolfe, and while it resounds with echoes of writers from Shakespeare and Sir Thomas Browne to Eliot and Scott Fitzgerald, Styron's indebtedness to Faulkner's *The Sound and the Fury* was all too evident. The manipulation of time, the multiple points of view, the interior monologues—even the plot, characters, and themes—were unmistakably Faulknerian.

Yet after all the labels had been pinned and all the influences noted, the critical consensus was that *Lie Down in Darkness,* while something of a *tour de force,* was not merely a twice-told regional tale of sound and fury. Admittedly its Southern setting had provided Styron, as he said in a *Paris Review* interview, with some wonderful material: for example, the "conflict between the ordered Protestant tradition, the fundamentalism based on the Old Testament, and the twentieth century—

8

movies, cars, television." Admittedly, too, it offered him a scene appropriate to a novel concerned with guilt and retribution, for as one of his characters says, the Southern " 'ground is bloody and full of guilt.' " Still, since guilt does not diminish nor moral paths perceptibly widen on the northern side of the Mason-Dixon line, one has to agree with Styron that his characters "would have behaved the way they did anywhere." And, one might add, at almost any time. On the one hand, *Lie Down in Darkness* exemplifies perfectly Nathan Scott's definition of the typical contemporary novel as one that deals with "the difficult marriage, the intricate maze of personal relationships within a family, the ambiguous sexual identity with all of its hazardous involvements, the crisis of self-recognition in middle-age." On the other hand, Styron makes these "fundamental human relationships . . . embrace the permanent truths of man's condition," a condition that in every age has produced feelings of faithlessness and despair.

The scene of *Lie Down in Darkness* is a land of dying, and the novel begins with a metaphor of spiritual dessication. Between the railroad station and the smoky industrial city of Port Warwick lies a desolate stretch of weeds and garbage heaps, with rusty gas-storage tanks towering above the wasteland. In the station Milton Loftis, Styron's heavy-drinking, self-indulgent, and spiritually bankrupt antihero, waits for a train bearing the coffin of his daughter Peyton, who has committed suicide in New York City and been temporarily buried in Potter's Field. Financially dependent on his estranged wife Helen, who despises him, and aware that his entire life has been a miserable failure, Milton had regarded Peyton as the one beautiful and somehow immortal part of him. Thus, her death not only marks the final stage in the disintegration of his family; it also forces Milton to confront his own mortality and to realize that life now holds absolutely nothing for him. The death of Peyton is, in effect, the death of her father as well, her burial the burial of Milton's last forlorn hope of finding some meaning in his stunted existence.

The journey from the railroad station to the cemetery constitutes the time-present of the novel. But as we move forward in space and time, listening with the mourners to a murmur of thunder both ominous and promising, we move simultaneously

9

into the minds of Styron's central characters—Milton, his mistress Dolly Bonner, Helen, the Reverend Carey Carr, finally Peyton herself. And through the reveries of each fractured consciousness, we are taken into the past preceding this terrible present. Just as the repeated breakdown of the cars in the funeral procession hint at the breakdown of the Americans' technological orientation when we are faced with the fact of death, so the disrupted temporal structure of *Lie Down in Darkness* reflects the spiritual and emotional disruption of a world in which propriety has replaced morality, lust has replaced love, and carefully tended houses and lawns disguise the spiritual disorder of their middle-class owners. The temporal disjuncture also corresponds to the waves of nostalgia that buffet the members of the Loftis family. Terrified by thoughts of a future even more painful than the present, they retreat into infantilism and into memories of that great good place of childhood innocence, harmony, and irresponsible self-indulgence from whence time has banished them. Milton's incessant sucking at whiskey bottles and his affair with Dolly Bonner, the childish woman who treats him like a small boy, are both defenses against the intolerable notion that life is meaningless and old age inevitable. Helen, too, dwelling on a time when she and Milton were still young, in love, and free of both knowledge and burdensome responsibilities, sucks persistently on cigarettes, pulls at her skin so that the wrinkles disappear, and thinks that the greatest gift of all would be never to have been born.

In trying to recover the past, however, the Loftises also uncover the sources of their present anguish and of the guilt that plagues them all. To Milton, morality is personified by the image of his dead father and by Helen, whom he sees through his father's eyes as the epitome of a Good Woman. To recall his childhood is, then, to recall the morality he has violated and the guilt he has incurred with his drinking and his adultery. This is why he is filled, on the day of Peyton's funeral, with a sense of long-prophesied doom. This is why he thinks of any disloyalty to Helen in terms of "schism and heresy." And this is why he prays, not to God, but to a father who will forgive his wayward son. Yet because this deified mortal had himself forsworn all but lipservice to Christianity, Milton has inherited only a vague moral squeamishness rather than a coherent ethic, gratuitous optimism rather than religious faith, and a habit of turning for solace and salvation to whiskey rather than to meditation and spiritual discipline. At the moment of his greatest anguish, therefore, he can only mumble, " 'I am the Resurrection and the Life.' What does that mean?" while his prayers, addressed with a lugubrious fervor to the empty skies, turn into parodies of themselves.

Whereas Milton's moral sense has no theological foundations, Helen's is based on a stern, though hazy, religious belief. Instilled by a commanding father, an archfundamentalist intolerant of all misconduct, it authorizes her inflexible ideas of right and wrong and explains her obsession with sin. But in the atavistic reaches of Helen's unconscious, her father is not only God's double, the being to whom she addresses her furtive apologies for sin; he is also the forbidden object of her sexual longings and consequently the cause of a terrible ambivalence. Because all desirable men are surrogates of the father whom she both loves and fears, sex to Helen can never be free of guilt. To confirm her own righteousness, she has projected this guilt onto Dolly (who, ironically, also identifies religion with her father), onto Peyton—in her mother's eyes a shameless seductress who is at once a reflection of Helen's repressed sensuality and a rival for the surrogate father's love—and onto the men who provoke her ambivalence. In Helen's nightmarish dreams her most powerful enemy, in fact, seems to be simply Man: her father, Milton, Carey Carr, even God Himself, those awesome figures possessed of the phallic power she both fears and lusts after, who clutter with filth the serene order of her house. However, the real antagonist of Helen's not so blessed rage for order is herself. As Peyton tells her during the violent confrontation between mother and daughter which climaxes the latter's wedding feast, " 'The terrible thing is that you hate yourself so much that . . . you hate everything.' "

Milton's spiritual emptiness and Helen's twisted religiosity— at best a plaything, at worst a hideous perversion—are undoubtedly among the things prompting William Van O'Connor's remark that *Lie Down in Darkness* is concerned with "the failure of Christianity, or with the inability of two generations, or more, to credit its validity." In a certain sense he is right.

11

Carey Carr, representative of the Church in the novel, admits that he could not nurture in Helen a truly Christian faith; he further admits that he himself feels at times "apostate," and abandoned by a God who declines to reveal himself. It seems to me, however, that Styron is less concerned with the failure of Christianity than with the tragic results of confusing things spiritual with things secular, things timeless with things temporal. Even Carr, who prides himself on his tasteful reconcilement of the secular and the sanctified, is subject to such confusion. Associating revelation with one beatific moment in his youth, he frets at his inability to attain a complete vision of God, and, like Helen, wishes everything could be absolutely identified as either vice or virtue. It is because Milton and Helen confuse God with their fathers, transcendent peace with the glory and the dream of a lost childhood, that they feel so abandoned, so bewildered, so repelled by their present existence. Yet Milton, at least, refuses to relinquish the illusion that paradise can be regained in the here-and-now, that by avoiding suffering and responsibility he can realize the Eden of his alcoholic dreams. Having only "toyed with the idea of grace," he dismisses it in favor of a misty beatitude induced by whiskey. Believing that he can rid himself of any uneasiness merely by talking, he substitutes meaningless conversation for confession, country club conviviality for religious communion, flirtation with Dolly for a confrontation with those psychic spectres of "things done, things undone" that might bring him understanding. When Ella Swan, the Negro maid, gives voice to these ghosts, Milton turns away— as he later turns away from the sight of Peyton's coffin, as he has always turned away from things disturbing and unpleasant.

The most flagrant of his evasions occurs when he deserts Helen and his other daughter, Maudie, to search for Peyton, who, unaware of her sister's impending death, is celebrating homecoming at a nearby university. In this instance, Milton is not only fleeing his responsibilities as a husband and father; he is also fleeing the fact of death to pursue something even he knows he cannot attain—the perpetual youth and immutable beauty embodied by Peyton. Searching vainly for her in that incongruous mixture of adolescent youth and regressively adolescent middle age that comprises a homecoming crowd, Milton is compelled at last to recognize his illusion for what it is, for he finds that youth and gaiety vanish whenever he comes upon them. Eventually he finds Peyton, but his drunken insistence that she wear his class ring only embarrasses her. She leaves, forcing Milton to confront that which he has always tried to avoid: the knowledge that his unpardonable sin is neither drunkenness nor adultery but apathy.

It is this same paralysis of the will that causes Milton at other times to suffer the existential nausea, to feel that he himself does not really exist at all, that only inanimate objects possess life and the "power to drive one witless with anxiety." Milton quite freely admits that he has never exerted his free will. He usually absolves himself, however, by recourse to a determinism based not on philosophical deductions or self-examination but on mental laziness and self-pity. Even in those undirected supplications which Milton substitutes for prayer, his request is not for the strength to transform himself but for a transformation miraculously to be wrought: "Ah, for a man to arise in me," he cries, "that the man I am should cease to be." Ironically, Milton gives the lie to his own denials of free will in the year following Maudie's death. He stops drinking, breaks off with Dolly, and tries to repair his broken marriage. And if this seems at first the result of some miracle, Carey Carr realizes that it is actually a consequence of a rare act of will on Milton's part. Unfortunately, this is the single "clock-tick of glory before the last descent" of Milton Loftis. Peyton's wedding, the irrevocable loss of one he loves in much more than a fatherly way, the very presence of youth in the air—all of these fill him with a curious passion which he cannot resist. To the accompaniment of church bells striking "reefs of recollection" in his mind, Milton lapses again into his dream of Eden. Sucking at his bottle, his lust for Peyton merges with memories of an Oedipal time, and his entire being becomes soft and damp and infantile.

Despite its brevity, Milton's short-lived assertion of will tempers our contempt for him. As Louise Gossett puts it, "Styron makes the helplessly weak person matter, not by arousing bathetic sentiment for him but by projecting his failure as a sign of . . . the frailty of man's will." Styron shows us Milton's fall; but he also asks, "do you know his wrassling?" We do, and are therefore persuaded that Milton has never been past redemption. It is more difficult to believe the same about Helen, who is as evasive in her own way as Milton. Her narcolepsy, her Nembutal-induced dreams of either flight or vengeance, her self-righteousness, are all defenses against life and others. And whereas Milton is merely afraid of life, Helen is "an incarnate No—reasonless and mute." True, she is in part the pathetic victim of a violated childhood and of marriage to a weakling; nevertheless, the fact remains that Helen, unlike Milton, willfully cherishes her wounds and her unswerving selfishness. Milton is weak of will and loves unwisely. Helen exercises her will in the service of hatred and vengeance, thereby destroying her capacity to love. She says she adored her father, but her dreams reveal that she hated him as well. She professes love for Milton, but prays for his emasculation and, failing that, his damnation. She insists that she loves God, yet ultimately declares that he is a " 'silly old ass,' " and she herself the possessor of a divine healing power which had lifted the fallen Milton from hell and "re-formed him in the image of decency, exalted him." Even her devotion to the crippled, feeble-minded Maudie is a twisted thing—as twisted, indeed, as its object. For Maudie, with her vacant, uncomprehending eyes, manifests that perpetual sleep which Helen herself would embrace. She is also totally submissive, and therefore—unlike Peyton—no threat to Helen's sovereignty.

Because God has ignored Helen's perverted prayers—not for guidance but for "reward and vindication"—she sells her soul to the devil. She knows that "by one word—Yes or Forgive or Love—she might have affirmed all, released all of the false and vengeful and troubling demons." But she refuses the Word, choosing instead to shelter the demons within her own bosom, to utter the everlasting nay, and to play the role of the serpent. She bites Milton, she bites herself, she bites Peyton.

Although Milton Loftis is the antiheroic hero of *Lie Down in Darkness,* Peyton is the center around which the action revolves. She is the catalyst of her parents' conflicts, and each of the major episodes in the novel takes place on a day of crucial importance to her: the Sunday that inaugurates Milton's fall from grace; her sixteenth birthday, which is climaxed by her discovery of Milton's affair with Dolly; the day of her departure for college, an occasion marred by the usual Loftis family quarrels; and the day of her wedding, which Carey Carr would like to think of as the "symbolic affirmation of a moral order" but which ends, like so many of the days of her life, in emotional chaos. In all these episodes, however, we see Peyton through the eyes of her parents. It is not until the day of her death, described in the novel's penultimate chapter, that Styron takes us into the mind of Peyton herself. Partly the ramblings of her unconscious and partly a kind of anguished meditation, Peyton's monologue virtually demands both Freudian and religious interpretations. For as Peyton moves through her final hours, her fragmented recollections and compulsively recurring images recapitulate those tormented, almost Aeschylean family entanglements that have made her what she is: a neurotic, irresponsible, sexually promiscuous yet guilt-ridden girl who seeks in death the peace and purification she cannot find in life.

Peyton is clearly the daughter of Milton and Helen Loftis. A spiritual orphan who feels that she is drowning in a sea of despair, Peyton too longs to be a child again, innocent and secure in a land " 'where a whimpering Jesus gently leads Winnie-the-Pooh down a lane of aching plum blossoms.' " Substituting the memory of a departed time for a concept of heaven, confusing herself or other humans with God, she can pray only to the lost part of herself, or to her father, or to Harry, her estranged husband, whom she identifies with her father and with God. And her prayer is always the same: that she be again as she was as a child, when she walked hand in hand with the father who is also lost to her now.

The loving and protective parent with whom Peyton associates her time of innocence is also the force behind its loss. When she realizes that he has "betrayed" her with Dolly Bonner, she seeks the arms of Charlie La Farge; and it is after Milton's homecoming debauch that she surrenders to Dick Cartwright. And she surrenders, not with passion or even defiance, but with a "peculiarly modern despair" which paints the two lovers "with fire, like those children who live and breathe and soundlessly scream, and whose souls blaze forever." As incapable of forgiveness as Helen, Peyton repeats this pattern after her marriage. Any suspicion that Harry has been unfaithful causes Peyton to regard herself as an Iphigenia whose father has sacrificed her to some stern goddess. It always sends her, even-

15

tually, into some other man's bed, there "to sin out of vengeance, to say, *so he doesn't love me, then here is one that will."* At another time she rationalizes her sins as attempts to find a new father and a home to replace the one she has lost. At still another time, however, she silently insists to Harry that she has lain down in the darkness only to punish herself for punishing him.

Whether Peyton's promiscuity is primarily a search for the father, an act of vengeance, or an inverted attempt at atonement, the images punctuating her monologue indicate that it is something beyond memory that impels her: namely, a complex set of partly repressed, ambivalent impulses associated with her past. All of them have to do with Peyton's Freudian involvement with her father. One of them occurred on a morning when Milton entered her room and kissed her awake. Alarmed by the latent passion underlying his playfulness, Peyton pushed him away. Another occurred on a day when Milton took the young Peyton up in a bell tower where the loud tolling of "Jesus Calls Me" and the noisy flight of pigeons had frightened the child. Clutching at his leg—a gesture she repeats as an adult whenever she is disturbed—Peyton fell into her father's arms. But when, overwhelmed by love, he held her close, she resisted him violently. A third experience took place after a school play in which, Peyton recalls, she had played the Spirit of Light. Wearing an almost transparent silver gown, she had climbed on Milton's lap and had noticed, as she jumped off again, that his face was "red and tense like a baby's when it goes off in its diaper." At the same time, he had urged her to be a "good girl" and reminded her, as his own mother had said, that "there'll be pie in the sky for them that keep their pants on." In the disorderly order of Peyton's mind, these dimly recalled but uncomprehended incidents are condensed into one. For in all of them her father appears as a god whose love she had simultaneously desired and repulsed, who had carried her "up and upward—oh Christ—when I was the Spirit of Light," yet who, along with the woman personifying morality to both of them, had warned her against the very sexuality he himself manifests and provokes.

The effect of these experiences on Peyton is self-hatred and a double-edged guilt: guilt for desiring her father and for having

16

denied him. To assuage the latter, she lies down in darkness with other "fathers." But in so doing, of course, she adds to that dirt underneath her bed which symbolizes the former. The hallucinatory birds that haunt Peyton like pursuing Furies are also emblems of guilt. Freudian images of orgasm, they appear whenever Peyton has any kind of sexual experience. Guilt is a winged thing—not only the birds that flew round the bell tower but the airplanes which, with wings like those of some predatory bird, Peyton associates with a night when she was punished by Helen. For Helen is an awesome Beatrice whose hands remind Peyton of white wings and whose scoldings were counteracted only when Milton lay down in the frightening dark with the crying child. But the "flightless birds" are also, as Maxwell Geismar points out, those "lonely souls which have suffered on this earth without soaring," an image which, at the last, Peyton tries to transform into that of an ascending and self-resurrecting Phoenix.

In the light of her conflicts, it is understandable that Peyton feels her soul to be "drowning out in dark space somewhere." Her fantastic dream of life inside a clock, "perfect and ordered and eternal," is a pathetic attempt to replace the God-deserted chaos of her temporal existence with a harmonious world of her own invention. In this universe of brass she would be free of desire, guilt, the "threat of hell," of time; here, she and Harry could "sleep forever," protected from both life and death. But when Harry fails to understand what the clock signifies to her, she throws it away, along with all her passion and dreams of order, and commits suicide.

In Freudian terms, Peyton kills herself because she is convinced that "all hope lies beyond memory, back in the slick, dark womb," and that "undivorced from guilt," she must divorce herself from life. That her guilt is connected with the paradigmatic episode of the bell tower is clear from the circumstances of her death. Removing her clothes so that she will be as naked and clean as a child, and answering the memory of her mother's moral warnings with a childish "oh pooh," she leaps from a loft in Harlem. She is delivering herself, she feels, into the arms of that god-father-lover who has betrayed her and has been rejected, in turn, by her. In other terms (as the pains in her womb ambiguously suggest), Peyton's suicide is not only an act of destruction but an attempt at re-creation. She hopes to find in death the all-powerful father she could not find in life. She also hopes to find her "light in ashes," to achieve in the darkness of physical death that birth of spirit aborted in temporality. Finally, by taking her faithless leap, she hopes to learn whether her redeemer does indeed exist, whether the distant thunder and equally "distant hallelujahs bare and absolute" are in fact signs that she will "rise again at another time and stand on the earth clean and incorruptible." For, like Faulkner's Quentin Compson, who commits suicide for much the same reason, Peyton is torn between belief and disbelief, between the feeling that God exists but (as Heidegger would say) is "withholding" himself and the feeling that God is nothing but a "gaseous vertebrate." The offspring, as she says, of a lost generation which lost its children, the dying Peyton can only pray for mercy "not because she hasn't believed but because she. No one. had a chance to. ever."

Unlike the characters in, say, Graham Greene's *The End of the Affair* or François Mauriac's *Viper's Tangle,* none of the Loftises—not even Peyton—comes to affirm God's existence as a consequence of sensing his absence. Helen ends apostate, Milton's eyes at the last are " 'those of a man who has gazed so long into the abyss that the abyss has begun to gaze back at him,' " and Peyton's final act is primarily a leap of despair rather than of faith. In fact, with the exception of Harry—whose painting affirms man's enduring capacity to create beauty and order even in the face of a Hiroshima—the only character in Styron's novel able to confront life without despair is the Dilsey-like Ella Swan. Wearing an expression beyond both grief and devotion, an expression which is simply "profoundly aware," Ella seems to have experienced everything and to expect nothing. Yet because her essentially tragic view of life includes a vision of Jesus, she has achieved a transcendent peace and can counter the Loftises' negations with an affirmative " 'Yeah! Yeah!' " This is not to say that Styron is offering the religion of Ella's Daddy Faith as a panacea or implying that blacks exist in a child's Garden of Innocence immune to the corruptions of white civilization. Daddy Faith is, after all, merely a Northern charlatan parading as a Southern savior; his revivalistic rite of rebirth, conducted as Peyton is being buried, is a grotesque

18

mixture of mythic, pagan, and Christian symbolism; and his sermon, a bizarre version of Peyton's tortured prayer and Harry's apocalyptic painting, evokes responses not altogether sacred. Daddy Faith is to La Ruth, Ella's daughter, what Milton is to Peyton: a demigod whose way leads to sexual satisfaction. Indeed, if the relationship between La Ruth and her mother is a "low comedy enacted . . . upon the stage of high tragedy," its resemblance to the relationship between Peyton and Helen suggests that pigmentation has nothing to do with guilt or innocence.

Styron declines, in fact, to assign any single cause or offer any simplistic solutions to the problems confronting his characters. Misunderstanding contributes, certainly, to the tragedy of the Loftis family. So do the debased values of their class and culture, their upbringing, their neuroses, their inherited frailties. Helen thinks God himself is at fault for blurring the distinctions between good and evil, and even Carey Carr implies at one point that God may be "the author of the original misdeed." But the fact remains that while circumstances have placed the family in a near occasion of sin, they themselves abuse the God-given will-to-choose that might have averted the tragedy. If they suffer from misunderstanding, too often it is because—out of fear or vanity or laziness—they deliberately avoid understanding, choosing instead to lie down in the darkness of nostalgia or forgetfulness or sensual indulgence. If the pain they inflict on others is frequently impelled by their own neurotic suffering, they also willfully refuse to give, to sympathize, or to control. The victims of both fate and character, they refuse in the long run even to live.

Christ on a Crutch: "The Long March"

—"Who really was a hero anyway, anymore?"

Written in Paris, where he was helping to found *The Paris Review,* Styron's *The Long March* (1953) is by his own account largely autobiographical. Like its two principal characters, Lieutenant Culver and Captain Mannix, Styron served in the Marine Corps during World War II and, as a reserve officer, was recalled to active duty in 1950 when the Korean War erupted. In the course of his nine-month hitch, he participated in the forced march on which the action of his second book is based. Because *The Long March* is a far less ambitious work than *Lie Down in Darkness,* it received less critical attention than Styron's first novel was accorded. It is not, for that matter, a novel at all. Only 120 pages long, it is an extended short story or novelette. Its structure and style are relatively spare and straightforward, although the evocative images that enrich *Lie Down in Darkness* are again evident. Despite its brevity and autobiographical base, however, *The Long March* is neither simple documentary nor what Malcolm Cowley calls a "tiny room in Bedlam." An outcry against the ceaseless war, the depersonalizing of persons, and the secularizing of spiritual authority in our time, *The Long March* also raises a more timeless question: what should a man do when confronted with those apparently irresistible forces that would not only control his body but break his will, subdue his spirit, and reduce him to robot-like obedience? Like Camus' *The Rebel* (which seems to have influenced *The Long March* as Freud influenced *Lie Down in Darkness*), Styron's book is about the necessity of rebellion and endurance in a world without God. And its central metaphor is that seemingly senseless and laborious " 'walk through the night' " that all men must take until they finally disappear into the universal darkness.

The irrational world of *The Long March* is epitomized in the first scene, a scene that is to haunt Culver and Mannix throughout and make the single day in which the book's action takes place seem absurd and unreal. A group of young Marines, just finishing their noontime meal, have been hit by a short round of mortar fire and are lying incongruously sprawled in a welter of blood and flesh and half-eaten food. Contemplating this slaughter of the innocents, a shocked and nauseated Culver realizes that it is simply a terrible accident. But why? And why in America, during peacetime? Mannix is comparably shocked. But to him, staring at a faceless youth who seems to retain, even in death, a "gawky, tousled grace," it is shock mixed with frustration, torment, and outrage. Sobbing, he cries out: " 'Won't they ever let us alone, the sons of bitches. . . . Won't they ever let us alone?' " If, as Camus says, "rebellion is born of the spectacle of irrationality, confronted with an unjust and incomprehensible condition," Mannix's rebellion commences at the moment when, in this gory noon, he confronts the spectacle of shattered youth.

For Mannix and Culver, two aging reserves recalled to the world of war, the entire training camp is a bloody wasteland which God seems to have abandoned. Their working hours are filled, as in a bad dream, with a frantic and fantastic chase after an invisible enemy, their leisure with the factitious luxury of an officers' club ironically dubbed "Heaven's Gate." Work and leisure alike seem unreal; yet in retrospect the years immediately following World War II appear to be only an idyllic dream of another kind. Like Peyton Loftis recalling her time of innocence, Culver associates his peacetime existence with a day at the end of childhood, a day that has irrecoverably vanished. And so, suspended between a present without sequence and a period that either "existed in the infinite past or, dreamlike again, never at all," Culver feels adrift upon a dark and endless sea. His quarters are a restricted, coffin-like universe; the radio signals resemble "cries of souls in the anguish of hell"; and the single light in his tent is as naked as the light . . . in an execution chamber." Mannix too is beset by feelings of constricted chaos, helplessness, abandonment. Untimely ripped from his womb of peace, he recalls a night during the last war when two drunken Marines had dangled him, naked and upside-down, from a hotel window two floors above the street. He feels as helpless now as he had then. And Culver, listening to Mannix's story, also suddenly feels "upturned drunkenly above the abyss . . . in terror clutching at the substanceless night."

In *Lie Down in Darkness,* the religious substance that might have illuminated and ordered the infinite darkness was either totally lacking or perverted. In *The Long March,* it has been replaced by a profane parody—belief in the supreme efficacy of military power. The spirit of this new religion is the famous Marine *esprit de corps*; its dogma is the new, the grandiose "amphibious doctrine"; its incantations are the gibberish of military passwords; and its ultimate aim is the "group destiny" of victory over its version of Satan, the "Aggressor Enemy." The institution supporting this theology of war is the Corps. The rock on which its temple is built, its high priest (even, perhaps, its god) is Colonel Rocky Templeton. Wearing a uniform as vestments and a gun as scepter, the Colonel is as filled with religious fervor as a priest, and sometimes looks, "like certain young ecclesiastics, prematurely aged and perhaps even wise." In fact, however, he is as mechanical as the machine he runs. With the chalky face of a mannequin-god and a solemn tone implying that he holds the answer to all questions, he responds to the accidental murder of the recruits as if he were receiving a routine message. Although Culver sees him as a kind of "priest in whom passion and faith had made an alloy . . . of only the purest good intentions," his acts are beyond the ordinary categories of good and evil. Ruler of a world that, in Camus' words, is "no longer . . . divided into the just and the unjust, but into masters and slaves," the Colonel's only values are strength, efficiency, and obedience. He is obeyed unquestioningly by officers such as Major Lawrence who, with his "baby-blue gaze and parted mouth" and "third-person flattery," is mechanical cherub to this mechanical god. He is obeyed by regulars such as Hobbs and O'Leary, whom the Corps "had molded . . . in its image" and who seem to have no existence outside the system. These obedient believers are immune to the god's wrath. But "with piety and with vengeance," he decrees damnation for a heretic such as Mannix.

When Templeton orders a forced march, partly as punishment for sins of the flesh (the flabbiness of the troops) and partly as preparation for some "humorless salvation," Mannix heretically and absolutely rebels. The object of his rebellion, however, is not Templeton the man, even though he mistakenly believes the Colonel's motives to be tainted by a cold and purposeful evil; its object is Templeton the Marine, representative of the absolute authority of a system whose values Mannix considers debased. Like the protest of Camus' absurd hero, Mannix's action has no calculated issue; it is "spontaneous protestation." Nor does he rebel by refusing to march. Instead, in "proud and willful submission, rebellion in reverse," he completes the hike—not because it is good or reasonable but simply to spite the system. Mannix thereby recants his earlier disavowal of " 'that Hemingway crap.' " For their determination "to last" is the distinguishing quality of Hemingway's spiritually triumphant Pilars and Manolos and Santiagos: the determination to exercise free will against forces that would suppress it.

Now for a while Culver regards the will to last as proof that they are *not* free, that they are "only marines, responding anew to the old commands." Free men, he thinks, would show their contempt for the whole business by dropping out. According to this logic, Mannix's defiance is both hopeless and absurd, his proud endurance futile in the face of a foreordained defeat. But Styron makes it clear that at this time Culver's mind is confused. To drop out would be (in Camus' terms again) absolute negation, renunciation as well as refusal. Mannix's will to resist, an assertion of the value of his personal existence, makes him *more* than a Marine; it makes him a man who, as Jerry Bryant has said, "imposes human meaning upon that which in surrender and despair would be meaningless."

It also makes him a hero. Perhaps, in a "generation of conformists" enslaved by a "horde of cunningly designed, and therefore often treacherous machines," he is only a hero of the absurd rather than a hero in the classical sense. Still, there have always been machines that would convert subjects into objects and destroy the apostate whose disavowals of faith threaten their sovereignty. History, in turn, has consistently awarded the role of hero to the man who prefers suffering to submission. Even the skeptical Culver recognizes that since suffering is implicit in the hero's role, Mannix is as heroic as anybody. Because he is human rather than divine, the Captain may be only a suffering buffoon; yet his scar and the contemptuous, wounded, but defiant look on his face suggest his kinship with other, more magnificent rebels. His nail-bruised heel, his refusal to honor the religion of the Corps, the great emptiness in his tormented soul, the "smoking bonfire" of his *hubris*-smitten spirit—all of these imply that he is a type of Satan or Old Adam to Templeton's God. As Peter Hays has pointed out, however, this thirty-year-old Jew is also a Son of Man to Templeton's Caiaphas, an all-too-human " 'Christ on a Crutch' " whose crucifixion began in the darkness of that noon when a drop of rusty blood from one of the massacred innocents stained his fatigues. Or perhaps it was foretold when Mannix's tone and words, in arguing with a superior officer, assumed the passion of an "absolute and unequivocal fact, as if they had been some intercession for grace." Until then, Mannix —as Camus says of his rebel at a similar stage—had at least remained silent, restricting himself to that "form of despair in which a condition is accepted even though it is considered unjust." Certainly the thirty-six-mile march, marked at each station by increasing pain from the nail in Mannix's shoe, recalls Christ's journey to the cross as well as the period of time from his death to his resurrection. When the Colonel finally condemns him to court-martial for overt insubordination, Mannix's face even takes on "an aspect of deep, almost prayerful concentration . . . so that if one did not know he was in agony one might imagine that he was a communicant in rapture." At this point Mannix has accepted the suffering implicit in finitude.

Although Culver finally persuades Mannix that the enlisted men should be allowed to ride the rest of the way, the Lieutenant's spirit sinks when Mannix agrees. " 'I've did—done. . . . To hell with them all,' " he says, as if giving up the ghost. Until then, despite a profound spiritual exhaustion, the Captain's huge, night-dominating voice has sustained Culver. It has sustained an entire company of reluctant Childe Rolands, driving them as with a "lash of thorns" to endure until the end. For to endure is to defeat the inhuman machine that would dominate them, while to get on the tempting truck "which would deliver them to freedom, sleep, oblivion" is to become less than the machine or, at best, no more than submissive animals. Mannix's hatred, his fanaticism, his bullying are at least manifestations of human concern. The Colonel, on the other hand, simply doesn't care. To him, "the hike had had nothing to do with courage or sacrifice or suffering"; he is an indifferent god, remote as the distant stars. Neither willfully evil nor willfully unjust, not even a tyrant, Templeton is simply "too conditioned by the system to perform with grace a human act" or to *"comprend"* (his own appropriately exotic word) a man such as Captain Mannix.

It is the implacability of a force wanting order at all costs that makes the Captain's contentions so agonizing and his dark face so like a tragic mask. It also contributes to the hunger for serenity that Culver, watching the mindless frolicking of the officers' wives, experiences after the march. Aware that "over distant peace and civilization, brewed the smoky and threatful beginnings of a storm," he almost envies the dead soldiers who are past caring. Mannix had cared. And now, still lost in the "never-endingness of war," he is faced with court-martial and the hell of Korea. Yet Mannix had completed the march and impelled Culver to do likewise. Refusing to submit to his own exhaustion, he had endured and ended as a man. To Styron, who has said elsewhere that any credo must end on the word "endure," that is evidently enough. For just as at the beginning of his story he juxtaposes the senseless slaughter of the young Marines with a glimpse of a blasted Negro cabin, so in his final scene he brings two representatives of racial endurance face to face. Naked except for a towel around his waist, Mannix the Jew encounters a black maid in the barracks hallway. With infinitely compassionate understanding she asks, " 'Do it hurt?' " —and then answers her own question, " 'Deed it does.' " Clutching a bar of soap denoting his purification, the man who had endured can only repeat " 'Deed it does.' "

The Existential Agony: "Set This House On Fire"

"We are serving our sentences in solitary confinement, unable to speak."

Set This House On Fire (1960), which is based in part on what has been called Styron's "saturnalian grand tour" of Europe in the 'fifties, is as long and convoluted as *The Long March* is short and straightforward. But whereas Norman Mailer's acerbic prediction that Styron's third book would be a suitably big and highly "literary" work may have proved true, the novel did not receive the enthusiastic reception Mailer anticipated. Some reviewers found it overblown and melodramatic; others thought its style pretentious, its character motivation vague and unconvincing; still others felt, with some justification, that it was merely a warmed-over mixture of the presently fashionable philosophies of Kierkegaard, Tillich, Heidegger, and Sartre. Yet if *Set This House On Fire* is not a perfect work of art, its imperfections stem largely, I think, from Styron's determination to grapple with profound moral issues and to express them in currently viable terms. And if the novel sometimes suffers from an overabundance of obtrusive literary contrivances—symbolic dreams, journal entries, parallels to *Don Giovanni, The Magic Flute,* and *Oedipus at Colonnus,* movements back and forth in time—this too results from Styron's effort to do full justice to the complexity of the issues.

As its motto from Donne indicates, *Set This House On Fire* is an apocalyptic picture of the world as purgatory, of man as the tormented inhabitant of a fiery house in which he struggles to attain redemption and a glimpse of God. Shortly after the novel begins, we are presented with a geographical metaphor of just such a spiritual condition. Port Warwick, Virginia, the setting of *Lie Down in Darkness,* is also the hometown of Peter Leverett, the admittedly "square" young lawyer who narrates *Set This House On Fire.* Streamlined, overrun by tract homes and commercial sprawl, culturally leveled by TV and the movies, Port Warwick has undergone a grotesque transformation since Peter's boyhood. Even the swamp where a Negro had once saved him from drowning and where he had first been made aware of his own mortality, is now the site of an Esso station. Peter is aghast at these changes; they make him feel totally estranged and robbed of all knowledge of his own identity.

Peter's father is equally disturbed by the changes. To him, they signify the general moral and spiritual decline into anarchy of a country where man is no longer the creature of God but a worshiper of Mammon. According to this angry and truly pious Jeremiah, America has become a nation of children in desperate need of tragedy, so that when they have " 'suffered agony enough and grief, they'll be men again.' "

Peter's father has spent his life searching for justice, for a Socratic harmony between himself and a morally ordered world. He has never found it. But perhaps, his son thinks, his failure matters less than that he sought and grieved and loved. Peter too is engaged in a search. Two years ago, in the Italian village of Sambuco, he had participated in the kind of tragedy his father has described, an experience that has contributed to Peter's present sense of estrangement. He has come South, in fact, to talk with Cass Kinsolving, another participant in the tragedy, in the hope that by penetrating the past he can come to terms with the present. The rest of the novel consists of conversations between Peter and Cass, interspersed with Peter's private recollections, during which the two men reconstruct the events in Sambuco and eventually recognize the significance of what happened there.

The experiences recreated for us by Peter and Cass are purgatorial from the start. On the night drive to Sambuco, Peter's car runs into a one-eyed peasant on a motor-scooter, and the accident leaves the American with guilt-feelings typical of his admitted tendency toward self-implication. On arriving in Sambuco, moreover, his sense of being adrift on a sea of blackness is compounded by an insubstantial dread that persuades him that hell may, after all, be a reality. For the little town strikes him as a barren place of "cataclysm and nightmare," a purgatory of tormented souls whose lamenting cries sound and resound through the ancient streets. Sambuco has its Casa Fausto, a hotel managed by the effeminate Fausto Windgasser. It has its devil-ridden Papageno in the person of the idiot Saverio. Most disturbing of all, it contains two manifestations of a corruption Peter had supposedly left behind: an American-owned villa resembling an Esso station, and an American movie company which remains in Italy for the sole purpose of using up *lire* credits. Here, mingling with Italians hot after a share of American opulence, are all the Hollywood types, native and otherwise: Carleton Burns, the foulmouthed matinee idol; Gloria Mangiamele, the brainless sexpot; Rosemarie Laframboise, a prototype of the standardized American female; Dr. Irvin Franklin Bell, the purveyor of popular religious pap who has made a fortune out of his "simple moral equation of wealth and virtue." Lost souls all, with the primal curse upon them, they have adopted as their Lord of Misrule the wealthy Mason Flagg, Peter's boyhood friend, the man who has invited him to Sambuco.

Peter and Mason had first met at St. Andrews (a prep school presumably modeled on Styron's own Christchurch). Into its pious Christian precincts, Peter recalls, Mason had "burst like some debauched cheer in the midst of worship, confounding and fascinating us all." And although Mason was soon banished from St. Andrews as hopelessly corrupt, Peter had been sufficiently captivated by him to renew their friendship later on in New York. Now, still captivated, he has accepted Mason's invitation to Sambuco. Peter eventually realizes that he had found Mason's very corruption insidiously tempting, his vain, handsome, arrogantly youthful face as beguiling as the fairseeming evil of a debased American Dream. Playing Nick Carraway to Mason's Jay Gatsby, Peter Leverett had reflected the approval Mason so desperately needs; he had appeased his friend's lust for ownership; and Mason, in turn, had exploited Peter's readiness to be owned.

Almost everyone at Sambuco, Peter discovers, is willing to be owned. They live off Mason's money and enjoy the supplies he obtains from a nearby PX, that miniature version of the Big PX that is America itself to the Italian peasantry. In return, the recipients of his generosity relinquish their souls to Mason, thereby providing him with the psychological nourishment he needs. For Mason, the apotheosis of Sartrean bad faith, can achieve a sense of identity only through other people. His autobiography is a fancifully constructed mosaic of others' experiences passed off as his own; and his professedly prodigious sexual activity is not an expression of his individuality and freedom, as he would have others believe, but merely the Don Juanian counterpart of his autoerotic obsession with cars and speed. To Mason, only literal or figurative rape—the forcible possession of one of his "dollbabies"—is satisfying. As Cass comes to realize, long after Mason's death, the latter sometimes seemed to be positively inhuman, a creature from some other world: " 'For him there was no history, or, if there was, it began on the day he was born. Before that there was nothing, and out of that nothing sprang this creature, committed to nothingness because of the nothingness that informed all time before and after the hour of his birth.' "

In one sense, Cass's description is of an inverted American Adam, a terribly vulnerable creature who is outside history not because he is innocent but because he is less than human. In another sense, however, it limns an American Satan let loose from Chaos to wander to and fro upon the earth. Mason does, in fact, share a number of characteristics with the Father of Lies. His lust to possess bears a "loathsome resemblance" to love; his apparently amazing erudition is actually only a matchless quackery; his charm is a mask for malice and poison on the one hand, for an abandoned innocence on the other. Even Peter—who should know that Mason is simply the pitifully forlorn product of a coldly authoritative father and a blindly indulgent mother—sometimes views him as an antichrist rather than as a mirror and a lure for one's own corruption. Cass, too, for a long while regards Mason as a positive force of evil; but then this self-educated, Southern-born American painter is a man peculiarly susceptible to Manichean visions.

As the suffering protagonist of *Set This House On Fire,* Cass Kinsolving stands somewhere between the antiheroic Milton Loftis and the almost tragic figure of Captain Mannix. Considering himself the evilest of men, he is actually a rogue-saint whose suffering, more than that of the other two, is of a kind describable in theological terms. With his Roman Catholic wife Poppy and their children, Cass lives beneath Mason's opulent villa in an unkempt apartment which reflects both a disorderly spirit and the artist's subjection to his dilettante landlord.

29

Fleeing a land whose ugliness poisons the soul, Cass has come from America to Sambuco by way of Paris, southern France, and Rome. But his flight has proved futile: he encounters Americans everywhere, their behavior reminding him that the country he cannot stop loving is a land of vulgarity and ignorance. Mason Flagg is the epitome of this warped and infantile culture, the very man Cass has come to Europe to escape. He is Evil Incarnate. And to this man the artist sells his soul. In return for food, medicine, and the liquor he cannot do without, Cass reduces himself to the level of an utterly dependent animal by painting a pornographic picture and performing clownishly obscene exhibitions for Mason and his guests.

The real causes of Cass's debasement, however, have very little to do with his exploiter. As the painter eventually realizes, Mason is not Satan; he is merely trash. The look of eternal damnation which Cass thinks he sees on Mason's face is a masked reflection of Cass's own self, a self so close to total corruption that it glories in being owned by the likes of Flagg. Nor can Cass blame America for what has happened to him. Its corruption is also a reflection of his own, his flight from the States a flight from that sickness unto death which he finally diagnoses and cures. Peter learns the history of Cass's illness during their conversations in South Carolina. According to Cass, its symptoms first became acute in Paris. Unable to work, he spent his time there drinking, whoring, and despairing over the talent that had apparently failed him. Then, at the very height of his prolonged debauch, he experienced an hallucinatory vision in which he seemed to perceive the otherness and the continuity of a cosmic, all-pervasive beauty. For the first time, as if he were peering into the face of heaven, Cass seemed to have grasped reality, including a sense of eternity and of selflessness. Although the vision was followed by nightmares of cataclysmic upheaval, Cass rationalized that ecstasy had to be paid for by an occasional confrontation of the abyss. Refusing to give up the self-destructive debauchery that produced his fantasy, he headed south, hoping that by approaching nearer the sun he could recapture the voluptuous beauty. So he came at last to Sambuco, where Peter Leverett beholds in him a man who has captured nothing but despair.

30

From the very beginning Cass had associated his aesthetic *satori* with another crystalline moment: a youthful sexual encounter with one Vernelle Satterfield, a nubile nymph who sold *The Watchtower* on streetcorners and seemed an immortal mixture of holiness and carnal reality. Just as Cass discovered, however, that Vernelle was not holy but merely a juvenile harlot whose " 'lust consumed all the simple piety in her eyes,' " so he ultimately realizes that his vision was nothing more than chemically-induced hallucination with no actual revelation about it. In short, he has mistaken a moment of Kierkegaardian "immediacy" for an unveiling of the absolute. His sense of transcendent selflessness and supernal knowledge vanishes with the vision, leaving him faithless and with an obsessive self-hatred.

As Kenneth Robb and Lewis Lawson have pointed out, Cass had suffered with Vernelle what Kierkegaard calls an unconscious despair; with the loss of his aesthetic vision, his self-love, and his faith, he suffers the double agony of a conscious despair. He knows that he has lost the grounds of a creative self and that the divine spirit has deserted him. He also knows that not to believe in some salvation is to suffer an anxiety approximating the pangs of hell. Yet he cannot conceive of being saved by a God whose shape seems impossibly mutable and elusive. To Cass, as to the characters in *Lie Down in Darkness,* God is sometimes a "disembodied gaseous vertebrate," at other times an omnipotent sadist who refuses to release his creatures from their agony. Capable of screaming " '*Dio non esiste*' " at one moment, Cass can nevertheless entertain the possibility that " 'God was not even a lie, but worse, that he was weaker even than the evil He created and allowed to reside in the soul of man.' " This last turns God—along with Mason, America, even Poppy's faith and selflessness—into a scapegoat for that sense of sin that produces in Cass the bestial desire for self-annihilation.

For a long while Cass fails to realize that self-loathing is itself a sin, that a denial of his potential goodness is a beast that one's ego-self erects between the soul and God. A prey of that beast, Cass finds all existence loathsome, and he longs, like Peyton Loftis, to lie down in the darkness of death. Only the fear of what eternity may hold in store tempers this yearning: fear of punishment for the forgotten crime that, heavily disguised, turns his dreams into nightmares of guilt and dread. When he associates the smell of hopeless poverty about the hovel of a tubercular Italian peasant with that of a Negro cabin he had once wantonly destroyed, he begins to understand his dreams as well as the source of his guilt and self-hatred. With that understanding, Cass takes the first step toward redemption. He devotes himself to the dying peasant Michele Ricci—who, except for his fantastic vision of an American paradise, is as faithless as Cass—and begins to emerge from the vortex of self into the knowledge that " 'hell is not giving.' "

Ironically, both Ricci and his daughter Francesca must die, and Cass must commit murder, before he can take the next step toward redemption. The agent of Cass's progress toward a state where dependence on Mason would be unthinkable, Francesca is nevertheless the human embodiment of Cass's aesthetic vision, the ideal of fleshly beauty which he has mistakenly substituted for faith. Echoing Kierkegaard's description of the "immediate" state, Cass says that he found in Francesca a joy which was " 'almost enough to preserve my sanity all by itself.' " But it is not enough. When Saverio murders Francesca and Michele dies raging against God, Cass feels that his last chance for salvation has been shattered; more than ever, he now perceives only universal nullity. Her death also causes him to perform an irrevocable act of violence. Believing Mason to be the one who has committed this abominable violation upon Beauty Incarnate, Cass stones Mason to death.

The discovery that Flagg, though guilty of rape, was innocent of murder forces Cass to the outermost edge of the yawning abyss. Yet it also moves him, in a roundabout way, a step closer to redemption. For in killing a man who seems the incarnation of moral outrage, Cass has at least taken (in Robb's words) the "Kierkegaardian leap from the aesthetic stage to the ethical stage"; he has reasserted his powers of moral choice; and he is now prepared to choose, once and for all, between Being and *il niente,* between the sin of self-destruction and an acceptance of that capacity for moral regeneration which, glimpsed in the face of the dying Mason Flagg, he has come to realize is present in all men. Although Cass's first impulse is to kill both himself and his family—the last because they are extensions of his detestable self—he overcomes that temptation with the help of Luigi Migliore, the Fascist-humanist policeman. Along with Leverett's father, Luigi is the philosophical oracle, the moral referee, at times almost the voice of God himself in *Set This House On Fire*. A Fascist for practical rather than ideological reasons, Luigi is also a mystic who has contemplated his own soul. Although he pessimistically proclaims that man is doomed to ultimate nothingness, he nevertheless retains his faith in the potential decency and perfectability of humankind. Luigi knows that the idiotic Saverio killed Francesca and that Cass killed Mason. But he conceals these facts from everyone except Cass; he persuades the guilt-stricken American that confession and imprisonment would not be acts of atonement but merely self-indulgent flights from the terror and anguish of being; and he convinces him that to wallow in remorse is a sinful denial of one's inherent goodness. Thus, with an " 'enormous and godawful solicitude,' " this unlikely angel of mercy allows Cass to " 'escape into freedom,' " where he can seek the courage to accept himself for what he is: a creature born to struggle against the evil and for the good within him.

Cass finds that courage. He returns to America, indicating by this acceptance and love of country that he has learned to accept and love himself as well. Free of the sinful guilt, the anxiety, and the despair that plagued him in Europe, he can now enjoy as much of life as is given him to enjoy. He can also help Peter come to terms with the South, with America (which, both men have learned, has no monopoly on corruption), and with himself. During the long conversation with Cass, Peter realizes that he, too, has been sinning in his egotistic guilt over the accident-prone Luciano and the self-doomed Mason. Indeed, by re-examining the past each man rises, like the recovered Luciano, from the ashes of his own malaise, and finds that he has freed himself from history in the act of accepting it.

Despite the Christian implications of all this, *Set This House On Fire* does not conclude by proposing theological answers to the problems it has posed. Cass admits that he is still puzzled about the sources and nature of evil: is it a cosmic force or entirely within man himself, reality or merely illusion, a sickness or something incurable which must be trampled upon? He is equally uncertain about the nature of God. Styron repeatedly reminds us, in fact, that both Cass and Peter are skeptical about the existence of a beneficent deity. With Luigi, they believe that all life is here and now, and that if God once existed he has long since departed, leaving only a black emptiness where he had been. Like Harry Miller, Ella Swan, and Al Mannix, Cass has endured. But beyond asserting that " 'ripeness is all,' " he declines to offer explanations, metaphysical or otherwise, for his endurance. He has returned from a state of living death; for the time being, " 'that would suffice.' " The philosophical center of the book from beginning to end is, then, simply the existential choice between Being and Nothingness in a world where progress from the ethical to the religious stage seems well-nigh impossible. Cass's final words to Peter are, in effect, Styron's final comments as well.

> "I suppose I should tell you that through some sort of suffering I had reached grace.... I wish I could tell you that I had found some belief....
> "But to be truthful...I can only tell you this: that as for being and nothingness, the one thing I did know was that to choose between them was simply to choose being, not for the sake of being, or even the love of being, much less the desire to be forever—but in the hope of being what I could be for a time."

History and Transhistory: "The Confessions of Nat Turner"

"He that overcometh shall inherit all things."

If *Set This House On Fire* was on the whole a disappointing book, *The Confessions of Nat Turner* (1967) has more than made up for it. Tantalized by an excerpt from the novel in the September, 1967 issue of *Harper's,* the public saw to it that Styron's fictional account of the only organized slave revolt in American history became an immediate bestseller; shortly after publication, Wolper Pictures purchased the movie rights to the book; and the reviews, in popular and literary magazines alike, have been almost unanimously laudatory. The praise is well deserved. In contrast to the philosophically cumbersome, aesthetically overblown *Set This House On Fire* and the moving but pyrotechnical *Lie Down in Darkness, The Confessions of Nat Turner* is marked by a restrained, confident manipulation of material which shows off Styron's enormous literary talents to the very best advantage. The imagery is brilliant but consistently functional, the pace urgent yet carefully controlled, the structure perfectly suited to the theme. The theme itself, of course, accounts for much of the novel's power. Indeed, to Philip Rahv, writing in *The New York Review of Books, The Confessions of Nat Turner* is the best novel by an American writer to have appeared in some years, principally because, in choosing Negro slavery as his subject, Styron has found that "mighty theme" so necessary to the creation of truly great fiction.

According to Styron, the theme had been ready to hand for some time. As a native of the Virginia Tidewater country where, in 1831, Turner's short-lived insurrection took place, Styron had at one time intended to make the "black John Brown" (as Edmund Wilson called him) the subject of his first novel. He is now convinced that would have been a mistake. If he had written it then, he says, "it probably would have been gothic." It would surely have lacked the perspective gained from Styron's twenty-year residence outside the South and from his observation of a more recent, more massive Negro rebellion. Finally, it would have lacked the most daring and brilliant feature of the book as we have it: the first-person point of view from which we see the novel's focal center—the mind of Nat Turner himself. Determined to confront directly the racial specter of his Southern heritage, Styron felt that for a man of his generation a third-person account would be both morally and artistically evasive. He had to understand the psychology of the black slave; he had to abandon the objective stance characteristically assumed by Faulkner, his literary master, in depicting Negroes; in short, he had to see and feel what Turner saw and felt.

This would be a job difficult enough for any white man, not to mention one living more than 130 years after the death of his subject. Styron's self-appointed task was made doubly difficult by the paucity of historical sources. Aside from a few contemporary newspaper articles and some skimpy court records, the only useful document of Turner's revolt is a 5,000-word pamphlet, "The Confessions of Nat Turner," dictated by the condemned slave to his court-appointed lawyer, Thomas Gray. From such a document (which Harriet Beecher Stowe had used in 1856 for her novel, *Dred*), Styron could not possibly discover the historical Nat's motives and modes of expression. But this very fact allowed Styron the freedom to infer them, to imagine what they were. Limited only by the novelist's commitment to plausibility, he could extend the psychological thrust of the work, expose the internal forces behind Nat Turner's revolt, and answer the question that Gray, inadvertently speaking for people like him in our own time, raises in Nat's cell: " 'How come you started a calamity like you done. . . ? How could the darkies get organized . . . and carry out such a plan?' " He could make Nat's language a vehicle for expressing complex emotions and for revealing the various and subtle demands endemic to a slave's condition—demands that lead Nat to speak to his white masters in an obsequious, whining dialect, to his fellow Negroes in the deliberately ambiguous language of an exploited and suspect people, and to himself and his God in an archaic, slightly courtly, but above all biblical language. Most importantly, Styron could turn the record of a single historical event into a "meditation on history": that is, he could show that an event that took place in the South more than a century ago, is in a sense not only repeating itself in the Detroits and Newarks of today but is analogous to still earlier events; that psychologically and spiritually, the past and present are one. For just as Nat Turner sees himself as a counterpart of both Christ and an Old Testament prophet, and the Negro slaves as counterparts of the ancient Jews in Egyptian bondage, so Styron implies that Nat is an early version of today's black militants. In so doing, he implies that the causes of Nat's rebellion were not so different from theirs.

As in *Lie Down in Darkness,* Styron's concept of time is suggested by the structure of his book. *The Confessions of Nat Turner* begins with the "Judgment Day" on which Nat receives his death-sentence. It then turns back by way of "Visions, Dreams, Recollections" to the "Old Times Past" of Nat's childhood and young manhood; it proceeds to "Study War," the story of the massacre; and it ends in "It Is Done. . . ," with Nat's execution. The metaphorical descriptions of early nineteenth-century Virginia also recall a technique common to Styron's earlier books. As Judge Cobb puts it, the state that was once the cradle of the nation is in his time rapidly becoming a wasteland, an empire converted into a breeding farm for the cotton kings of the Deep South. This is the ruined land that produces Nat Turner, son of a rebellious runaway slave whom he never knew and of a mother who cooks in the white man's kitchen. Personifications of the past, Nat's parents contribute prominently to the formation of his attitudes. He presumably inherits his rebellious pride from his father, and he acquires from his mother a contempt for the field Negroes. But that proximity to the white world by which he measures his superiority makes him at the same time paradoxically aware that master and slave, whether field hand or domestic servant, are subject to the same human frailties. When a drunken white overseer sexually assaults Nat's mother, the child is as struck by his parent's partial acquiescence, even collaboration, in her own debasement as he is by the overseer's brutality. When, as an adolescent tortured by his own desires, he overhears the profane words and uncontrollable passion of a white woman he has formerly regarded as saintly, he is further convinced that bestiality is not peculiar to black field workers or socially inferior whites. Close contact with his nominal superiors is, then, not only the soil in which the seeds of his ultimate hatred take root; it is also the ground of his determination to deny the flesh and rise above both the blacks and the whites of his world.

Belief in his exalted nature takes firm hold when Master Samuel Turner makes him the subject of a singular experiment: he is taught to read. (In the light of future events, it is ironic that the first literature to which Nat is exposed is Bunyan's *The Life and Death of Mr. Badman,* a book he steals from Turner's library, leaving behind its companion volume, *Grace Abounding*!) Thereby raised even further above his fellow slaves, Nat trembles with the glory of self. Like Jesus in the temple, he astounds his pharasaic elders with his knowledge of Scripture and conceives the notion that he is a creature of rare gifts and divinely inspired insights. His unconscious identification with the Son of God is subtly reinforced later on. Taught carpentry by one Mr. Goat, a German whose name must really have been "something like Godt," he accidently punctures his hands with a drill, thereby foreshadowing his crucifixion.

Until Nat accepts his spiritual kinship with other slaves, however, he is a messiah without a people to save. This is accomplished through a homosexual experience with Willis, the first Negro for whom Nat has felt any real affection. To Nat, obsessed with religion and given to spiritual interpretations of the most mundane events, the act is a symbol of communion with all his black brothers. He follows it by performing his first baptism. Although this last confirms his sense that he has been singled out by God for some holy purpose, the sexual ecstasy itself convinces him that if he is to consecrate himself to God's service, he must in future avoid all such fleshly pleasures. From this point on, Nat's sexual and religious feelings are inextricably intertwined. To control his physical desire, he goes into the wilderness for periods of prayer and fasting during which erotic fantasies are confused with religious visions, and images of rapturous intimacy with white women are increasingly replaced by images of their violation. Because both society and conscience prevent Nat from having what he so urgently wants, he would destroy what he wants, especially those women whose pity and sympathy both inflame his passion and sharpen his anguished awareness of their inaccessibility.

Willis is also an involuntary goad to Nat's destructive impulses. For reasons of economic necessity, Turner sells Willis to a slave trader; Nat, consumed by fury and convinced that he has been betrayed, banishes his veneration for Turner. More betrayals follow, each one strengthening his conviction that white men are incorrigibly duplicitous. Rather than freeing Nat as he had promised, Turner delivers him into the temporary custody of the Reverend Mr. Eppes, a homosexual preacher and incarnation of evil. According to the well-intentioned but shortsighted Turner, Eppes has agreed to free Nat after a short period of time. He never honors that agreement. Instead, releasing Nat from a purgatorial state between bondage and the promised liberty, Eppes introduces him to the hell of total, hopeless slavery. In this satanic domain, the skull beneath the skin of a system-serving Christianity is laid bare by the Babylonian mockeries of the tormented and tormenting Eppes. In this domain, too, Nat is fully transformed from a black Christ into a black angel of vengeance.

Nat passes eventually into the comparatively benevolent hands of Joseph Travis, who on occasion hires him out to the Whitehead family. Richard Whitehead is a minister of the gospel whose demon-ridden face reflects a religious inversion equal to Eppes's. His sister Margaret, on the other hand, is a being such as Nat has never known before. Giddy, sentimental, unaware that her carelessly exposed body inflames Nat, she nevertheless manifests a truly Christian *caritas*. For Nat the die is cast. Because the desire he feels for this veritable Little Eva can be neither appeased nor converted into love, the sympathy that flows between the slave and the white missy seems merely an unwanted mitigation of his rage, her compassion a lure of Satan rather than of Christ. Indeed, pity, sympathy, and improved conditions paradoxically fan the fires of Nat's hatred and increase his passion to destroy the white devils who possess him. Styron's protagonist resolves that paradox, if not for Gray and the other white people of the time, for himself and for us. The fiery crux of a Negro's existence, he explains, is that if you "tickle him with the idea of hope . . . he will want to slice your throat." Like the Negroes of our own time, Nat has been tickled with hope; and when the hope proves false, the primary objects of his rage are the white liberals who tickled him. Combined with a partial education less bearable than none at all, and with erotic energies that can find their only outlet in violence, Nat's frustrated hopes assume a new shape: a carefully formulated plan for violent vengeance.

Thinking himself a second Christ preparing a holy war against Satan, Nat sets out to recruit disciples from among his downtrodden people. But while he tells Margaret that his favorite psalm is the one beginning "Be merciful unto me," Nat hones himself into an instrument of wrath rather than of mercy. He is a savior who advocates not peace but a sword, a revolt not of the spirit but of the flesh. For to Nat, so sorely sinned against, all nature is charged not with the grandeur of God but with the abominations of a generation of white vipers. Nor, coming increasingly to believe in his infallibility and omnipotence, does he advocate humility. In the words of an antebellum Malcolm X, he imbues his disciples with the spirit of black militancy, converts Napoleon, Joshua, David into Negro heroes bestriding the carnage of the white world like apocalyptic angels, and preaches that only an everlasting pride will make them free. It is not the language of the suffering servant which inspires Nat and the followers he slowly gathers around him; it is the language of the Old Testament prophets—Ezekiel, Daniel, Isaiah, and Jeremiah. He conceives of his plan to destroy all the whites in the community, and hence inspire blacks to revolt throughout the South, as a fulfillment of Isaiah: *"To loose the bonds of wickedness, to undo the heavy burden, and to let the oppressed go free, and that ye break every yoke."* He feels the closest kinship to the divinely furious Ezekiel. And his visions, recalling Cass Kinsolving's horrendous nightmares, are not of tranquillity and unity but of a great gaping rupture of the heavens, out of which a black angel emerges to vanquish a pure white antagonist. Echoing Daniel and Revelation rather than the Gospels, the primal source of these visions is not, of course, the Bible at all but the satanic forge within Nat's own tortured soul.

Eventually Nat admits that God had in fact spoken only two words to him: " 'I abide.' " Like his spurious apocalypses, Nat's "voices" are hallucinations brought on by fasting, religious mania, and sexual deprivation; they are the slavery-induced voices of fury, frustration, and a passion for vengeful justice. Psychologically, however, Nat must convince himself that his cause is just and his bloody plan divinely sanctioned. Not so with his disciples. Nelson, for example, joins Nat's band simply because he thinks that it *"mought make a nigger worth somethin' to hisself, tryin' to get free, even if he don't."* Others—less concerned with human dignity—are so "bedeviled, torn apart by hatred, sick unto death of bondage [that] they would have cast their lot with the most evil ha'nt or phantom of the woods to be shut forever of the white man's world." Even Hark, a majestic figure in contrast to those Negroes reduced by slavery to the state of abject and docile animals, is entirely free of Christian scruples and restraints; in fact, he considers the infernal conditions of slavery quite possibly the invention of a malevolent God, and regards as the agent of a cosmic cruelty the white master who has separated him forever from his wife and child. The murderous Will, on the other hand, is indifferent to all speculation. Little more than an animal underneath a "carapace of scarred black skin," Will impresses Nat as being an "inchoate universe of hatred" whose urge to destroy embraces every living thing. Will is an avatar of the brute in all men, including Nat, and the necessary instrument of the latter's plan to redeem the Harks of the race. Yet he is also the greatest threat to the plan, for as the human analogue of the "beast dreadful and terrible," he is capable of turning dream into nightmare, redemption into damnation, spiritual triumph into spiritual failure.

The rebellion does fail, both materially and spiritually. First of all, Nat's plan for taking the town of Jerusalem (now called Courtland) is naively based on the military strategy of Joshua and David, and this alone makes failure inevitable. Furthermore, once the massacre has passed its crest, Nat's disciples betray their leader with drunkenness, cowardice, and dispersal. Finally—and to Nat, the most crushing blow of all—the majority of the slaves, far from joining in the uprising, defend their white masters against the insurrectionists. Both materially and spiritually, however, the rebellion fails because at the moment when action is most imperative, Nat is unable to act. He is suddenly overwhelmed by the fact that Travis, who was to be his first victim, is not some abstract instrument of bondage but a man like himself. Nat cannot kill him. He can only yearn to flee into the wilderness, hide himself from the eyes of God and man alike, and leave the killing to Will. Nat does not flee, but by the time he commits his first and only murder, he has long since effectually relinquished his role of leader to Will. Later on, moreover, he spares a young girl who is to sound the alarm against his army. Hence, the very quality that makes Nat morally superior to Will allows the latter to replace him as the "black avatar" of freedom. The very quality that makes him superior to his masters, the understanding that a man is neither an object nor an abstraction, leads to his defeat at their hands.

Appropriately enough, the two-day blood bath which destroyed fifty-five white persons ends in a cave in the Dismal Swamp. For the dark and treacherous forest where Nat is captured is a fitting emblem for the bog of despair, the cave of error, the jungle of tangled emotions in which his mission had been conceived. It is equally fitting that his death sentence

41

should be pronounced by Judge Jeremiah Cobb, the one white man Nat had intended to spare. A lordly figure who, long ago, had spoken to Nat in prophetic tones of the doom awaiting his beloved state of Virginia, Cobb had seemed as ravished by sorrow and injustice as any slave, and therefore as deserving of mercy. In Nat's eyes, Cobb's awesome stature increases during the trial. Still thinking himself a Christ, the presence of whose "body in custody had been verified," Nat views Cobb, not as a Pilate in an hysterical Jerusalem, but as a Father-God condemning his Son to a foreordained crucifixion. Like some predestinating yet grieving deity, the Judge seems to regard Nat from "immeasurable distances" with eyes that, "profound as all eternity," suggest that he shares with the condemned man a "secret—unknown to other men—of all time, all mortality and sin and grief."

Surely this remote and cadaverous surrogate divinity is closer to Nat than God himself. For the man who thought himself a saint is now if anything one of Camus' saints without God. Gazing at the indifferent dark falling inexorably over Jerusalem, Nat finds himself unable to pray. Like Cass Kinsolving, he is consumed by a nauseous despair verging on, yet lying deeper than, madness. Earlier, Nat had thought of his fellow slaves as existing in a state little better than that of a will-less fly. Now he himself seems to be on the brink of that "ultimate damnation": to be—if not one of "God's mindless outcasts"—a creature whom he has forgotten, "with a forsaken solitary apartness so beyond hope that I could not have felt more sundered from the divine spirit had I been cast alive like some wriggling insect beneath the largest rock on earth, there to live in hideous, perpetual dark."

Nat's sole companion at this point is Thomas Gray. And the lawyer, like Rubashov's Ivanov in *Darkness at Noon,* is at best a devil's advocate, at worst a type of antichrist. In either case, he is a false prophet. Insisting that Negroes are incapable of revolution, he predicts that slavery will last for a thousand years, that Nat's slaughter of the innocent and not-so-innocent alike has in fact insured the absolute defeat (rather than, as Styron himself believes, merely the delay) of abolition. Ridiculing Nat's faith in divine guidance, he proceeds to argue that Christianity is finished and that God is a lie. Nat is severely tempted to believe this incarnate Spirit of Denial. Perhaps, Nat thinks, "God is dead and gone, which is why I can no longer reach him." But Nat also suspects that he may have removed *himself* from God's presence, that he has been wrong from the start, and that the intolerable emptiness he feels stems from his lack of remorse.

Nat had first noticed God's departure immediately after the start of the uprising. He had reflected then that perhaps this was God's way of forcing him to consider things he had not thought of before. One of the things he had not thought of is the possibility that the massacre is a Black Mass rather than a divinely guided Act of Atonement. Another is the possibility that spiritual liberation and fulfillment lie elsewhere, that even now, in his dark cell of despair, there is still "one hostage for his soul's ransom." In the infinite sense, the hostage is Christ, incarnation of the love and mercy Nat has forsworn; in the finite sense, it is Margaret Whitehead, the only one whom he wishes he had saved, and who—in an almost miraculous way—now saves him. For as Nat finally realizes, the girl he had thought merely sentimentally pious had after all shown him "One whose presence I had not fathomed or maybe even known." Because he had simultaneously loved her for her beauty and goodness and hated her for being beyond his reach, her murder had been both a sexual act (*"Ah, how I want her,* I thought, and unsheathed my sword") and an inverted religious sacrifice of the one being standing between him and an unqualified hatred of white humanity. Because she had looked at her murderer forgivingly, Nat had felt compelled to make an "ordained circuit of her body," as if that object clad in the virgin's blue were the center of some "ceaseless pilgrimage." And because his feeling of inconsolable loss is somehow tied up with memories of her death, he begins to understand dimly that only by repenting that death can his emptiness be a vessel for God's grace. Finally, in a masturbatory fantasy approximating a profane act of meditation, Nat attains an ecstatic vision in which he and Margaret, the "twain—black and white—are one." Almost concurrently he remembers the words of Christ she had once recited to him: *"Beloved, let us love one another for love is of God; and everyone that loveth is born of God and knoweth God."* With this revelation of love and union, Nat Turner

43

moves beyond both rage and despair; the God whose name he had nearly forgotten returns; and he dies the death thinking of the "bright and morning star." Thus Styron's story, which evolved slowly but inexorably toward the furious crescendo of the massacre, ends on a decrescendo of transcendent serenity and equilibrium. It ends, in fact, almost as it began—with Nat's paradigmatic image of a "white inscrutable . . . mystery"— except that at the last the image is accompanied by Christ's words: "Then behold I come quickly."

Although Nat's death-dream of a supernatural marriage with the lily-white Margaret (*"We'll love one another by the light of heaven above"*) may seem distressingly similar to Fenimore Cooper's conveniently posthumous consummation of the love affair between Uncas and Cora, the dream is perfectly consistent with Nat's psychology as revealed in the rest of the novel. It is certainly not offered as a solution to racial problems. Styron offers no solutions. Perhaps, as James Baldwin has said, *The Confessions of Nat Turner* is a "hopeful book" in that it "attempts to fuse the two points of view, the master's and the slave's." Hark's final assurance that everything will eventually come right, and the pity Nat feels for the benighted Gray when, for the first and last time, they shake hands—these too hint at Styron's faith in something other than a transhistorical reconciliation of black and white. On the other hand, by revealing both the consciousness of a Negro slave and those upsurges of the collective white unconscious in which "animate chattel" exercise their powers of moral and spiritual choice by destroying their owners, Styron seems to be uttering a prophetic cry of another sort as well. Giving the lie to America's faith in a linear, self-consuming historical progression, he has issued to black and white together a familiar warning: that those who are heedless of the lessons of history are doomed to repeat its mistakes.

Styron has described *The Confessions of Nat Turner* as a "kind of religious allegory" in which "Old Testament savagery and rage" are converted at the last into "New Testament grace and redemption." His previous novels are by no stretch of the imagination religious allegories. Yet the crucial importance of religion in all of them is undeniable. Styron's symbolism, while too complex and contextually naturalistic to be called allegory,

44

nonetheless consistently includes a religious dimension. His biblical allusions and metaphors, the carefully established parallels between his characters and their actions and those of the Judeo-Christian *mythos,* his repeated (if sometimes ironic) references to grace, beatitude, redemption, damnation—all these betoken a fundamental, not to say sectarian, interest in theology. Nor are they merely techniques by means of which Styron has attempted to invest his fiction with a spurious universality and meretricious high seriousness. They are, instead, both vehicles of and signs pointing toward his principal subject: man's struggle to find spiritual sustenance in the God-forsaken wasteland of modern life.

Styron is obviously aware that ours is not the only age in which men have experienced the absence of God. In *The Confessions of Nat Turner*—which, for all its contemporary parallels, takes place in the nineteenth century—Nat remarks to Lawyer Gray that God has frequently hidden himself from our sight, "so that long periods on earth would pass during which men might feel that He had abandoned them for good." But Styron, like so many other contemporary writers, also clearly believes that mid-twentieth century men feel this abandonment with particular intensity. Consequently, as Luigi Migliore puts it, they " 'can only leave notes to him—unread notes, notes that mean nothing.' " Neither Luigi nor Styron can explain why this has happened. They only know that it is our condition and our curse, and that while we wait for his return, " 'we do what we can.' "

If Styron cannot explain why it has happened, he has at least written notes that mean a great deal. His typical protagonist cannot offer systematic explanations either, theological or otherwise. But what that protagonist *can* do, he finds, is wrestle with the blackness and resist the embrace of nihilism. In other words—Styron's own—his books are all "predicated on revolt in one way or another." Milton Loftis rebels, however briefly and unsuccessfully, against his own moral paralysis; Al Mannix rebels against a system that, in the name of order and a violent collective destiny, would possess his soul and enslave his will; Cass Kinsolving rebels against a nihilistic spirit of denial and against the void itself; Nat Turner rebels against an injustice that mocks the very name of God. Whatever form it takes, however, the rebellion is an essentially metaphysical struggle to affirm meaning in a world that denies it. All the characters, at one time or another, suffer the sickness unto death; but with the possible exception of the pitiful Milton Loftis, all of them endure and overcome their despair.

Now it may be, as Cass says, that this is " 'not a matter of being Christian' " but simply a matter of endurance for its own sake. Yet it may also be, as Styron suggests at the end of his latest and most magnificent novel, that "he that overcometh," thereby asserting his full humanity, "shall inherit all things" and find that God is not absent after all. For a writer in our time, perhaps suggestion will have to do; perhaps it will have to suffice.

SELECTED BIBLIOGRAPHY

Note: The most comprehensive list of writings by and about Styron is to be found in David D. Galloway's *The Absurd Hero in American Fiction*.

BOOKS BY WILLIAM STYRON

The Confessions of Nat Turner. New York: Random House, 1967.
Lie Down in Darkness. Indianapolis: Bobbs-Merrill, 1951.
The Long March. New York: Random House, 1956.
Set This House On Fire. New York: Random House, 1960.

CRITICAL AND BIOGRAPHICAL STUDIES

Aldridge, John W. *In Search of Heresy: American Literature in an Age of Conformity.* New York: McGraw-Hill, 1956, pp. 126-148.
Arnavon, Cyrille. "Les romans de William Styron," *Europe,* XLI (September, 1963), 54-66.
Baumbach, Jonathan. "Paradise Lost: The Novels of William Styron," *South Atlantic Quarterly,* LXIII (Spring, 1964), 207-217.
Benson, Alice R. "Techniques in the Twentieth Century Novel for Relating the Particular to the Universal: *Set This House On Fire,*" *Papers of the Michigan Academy of Science, Arts, and Letters,* XLVII (1962), 587-594.
Bonnichon, Andre. "William Styron et le second Oedipe," *Etudes,* XIII (October, 1962), 94-103.
Brandriff, Welles T. "The Role of Order and Disorder in *The Long March,*" *English Journal,* LVI (January, 1967), 54-59.
Bryant, Jerry H. "The Hopeful Stoicism of William Styron," *South Atlantic Quarterly,* LXII (Autumn, 1963), 539-550.
Cheyer, A. H. "William Styron," *Wilson Library Bulletin,* XXXVI (April, 1962), 691.
Davis, Robert Gorham. "The American Individualist Tradition: Bellow and Styron," in *The Creative Present: Notes on Contemporary American Fiction,* ed. Nona Balakian and Charles Simmons. Garden City: Doubleday, 1963, pp. 111-141.
Davis, Robert Gorham. "Styron and the Students," *Critique,* III (Summer, 1960), 37-46.
Detweiler, Robert. *Four Spiritual Crises in Mid-Century American Fiction.* Gainesville: University of Florida Press, 1964, pp. 6-13.
Fenton, Charles A. "William Styron and the Age of the Slob," *South Atlantic Quarterly,* LIX (Autumn, 1960), 469-476.
Finkelstein, Sidney. *Existentialism and Alienation in American Literature.* New York: International, 1965, pp. 211-242.
Foster, Richard. "An Orgy of Commerce: William Styron's *Set This House on Fire,*" *Critique,* III (Summer, 1960), 59-70.
Friedman, Melvin J. "William Styron: An Interim Appraisal," *English Journal,* L (March, 1961), 149-158, 192.

Galloway, David D. *The Absurd Hero in American Fiction: Updike, Styron, Bellow, Salinger.* Austin and London: University of Texas Press, 1966, pp. 51-81.

Geismar, Maxwell. *American Moderns: From Rebellion to Conformity.* New York: Hill and Wang, 1958, pp. 239-250.

Gossett, Louise. *Violence in Recent Southern Fiction.* Durham: Duke University Press, 1965, pp. 117-131.

Gresset, Michel. "Sur William Styron," *Mercure de France,* CCCL (February, 1964), 297-303.

Hassan, Ihab. *Radical Innocence: Studies in the Contemporary American Novel.* Princeton: Princeton University Press, 1961, pp. 124-133.

Hays, Peter L. "The Nature of Rebellion in *The Long March,*" *Critique.* VIII (Winter, 1966), 70-74.

Klotz, Marvin. "The Triumph over Time: Narrative Form in William Faulkner," *Mississippi Quarterly,* XVII (Winter, 1963-1964), 9-20.

Lawson, John Howard. "Styron: Darkness and Fire in the Modern Novel," *Mainstream,* XIII (October, 1960), 9-18.

Lawson, Lewis. "Cass Kinsolving: Kierkegaardian Man of Despair," *Wisconsin Studies in Contemporary Literature,* III (Fall, 1962), 54-66.

Matthiessen, Peter, and George Plimpton. "The Art of Fiction V" (an interview with Styron), *Paris Review,* No. 5 (Spring, 1954), 42-57.

McNamara, Eugene. "William Styron's *Long March*: Absurdity and Authority," *Western Humanities Review,* XV (Summer, 1961), 267-272.

Moore, L. Hugh. "Robert Penn Warren, William Styron, and the Use of Greek Myth," *Critique,* VIII (Winter, 1966), 75-87.

Mudrick, Marvin. "Mailer and Styron: Guests of the Establishment," *Hudson Review,* XVII (Autumn, 1964), 346-366.

Nigro, August. *"The Long March:* The Expansive Hero in a Closed World," *Critique,* IX (1967), 103-112.

O'Connell, Shaun. "Expense of Spirit: The Vision of William Styron," *Critique,* VIII (Winter, 1966), 20-33.

O'Connor, William Van. "John Updike and William Styron: The Burden of Talent," in *Contemporary American Novelists,* ed. Harry T. Moore. Carbondale: Southern Illinois University Press, 1964, pp. 205-221.

Robb, Kenneth A. "William Styron's Don Juan," *Critique,* VIII (Winter, 1966), 34-46.

Rubin, Louis D., Jr. *The Faraway Country.* Seattle: University of Washington Press, 1963, pp. 185-230.

Scott, James Burton. *The Individual and Society: Norman Mailer vs. William Styron* (unpublished dissertation). Syracuse University, 1965.

Stevenson, David L. "Styron and the Fiction of the Fifties," *Critique,* III (Summer, 1960), 47-58.

Urang, Gunnar. "The Broader Vision: William Styron's *Set This House on Fire,*" *Critique,* VIII (Winter, 1966), 47-69.